Presented to

_____

_____

on

_____

_____

by

_____

_____

_____

EDICATION

This book is dedicated to my dear brother, Dr. Clarence Sexton, who prayed for my salvation for many years, and who *"...first findeth his own brother..."* and brought me to Christ.

I saw in his life what a five star Christian was, and he challenged me to become one.

The Lord Jesus has shown me that if Christians will do five things and do them consistently, they will have power to become what God has redeemed them to be. A statement that you will read often in this book is:

> Victory in the Christian life comes by doing these five things consistently; failure and defeat can be traced to the neglect of one or more.

May the Lord Jesus help all who know Him to become five star Christians.

Tom Sexton

John 8:29

Becoming a
FIVE STAR CHRISTIAN

Dr. Tom Sexton

Becoming A Five-Star Christian

2nd Edition
Copyright © 2024 Dr. Tom Sexton

Published by Five Star Christian Ministries
Cape Coral, FL
WordToTheWorld@aol.com
www.FiveStarChristianMinistries.com
ISBN: 979-8-9905333-6-3

All Scripture quotations are from the Authorized King James Bible.

Printed in the United States of America

Contents

The disciples, along with the first century believers, were five star Christians.
The result was that they grew in the Lord Jesus, they had the favour of God on their lives, and the Lord added to the church daily.

$\mathcal{B}$ecoming a
FIVE STAR CHRISTIAN

Three times the word *"Christian"* appears in God's Word.

*"If any man suffer as a **Christian**, let him not be ashamed; but let him glorify God on this behalf"* **(I Peter 4:16)**.

*"The disciples were called **Christians** first in Antioch" **(Acts 11:26)**.*

*"Agrippa said unto Paul, Almost thou persuadest me to be a **Christian" (Acts 26:28)**.*

Becoming a Christian is a life-changing decision. The change takes place on the inside and transforms the life from the inside out. Religion tries to change man from the outside in, but only Christ can change a man from the inside out.

This change can take place as simple as the ABCs.

 **Acknowledge** that you are a sinner. *"For all have sinned, and come short of the glory of God"* **(Romans 3:23)**.

 **Believe** that the Lord Jesus died for you. *"But God commendeth His love toward us, in that, while we were yet sinners, Christ died for us"* **(Romans 5:8)**.

 **Call** upon the Lord to save you. *"For whosoever shall call upon the name of the Lord shall be saved"* **(Romans 10:13)**.

You become a Christian by turning to God in repentance and faith, and receiving the Lord Jesus as your personal Saviour.

If you have never received Christ as your personal Saviour, pray and receive Him today.* Then join a Bible-believing church and determine to become a five star Christian.

* For more on receiving Christ, turn to page 91.

The Christian life is a learning and growing process. The Bible says to *"add to your faith"* (**II Peter 1:5-7**). Each star represents an ingredient that we should add to our lives to be our best for our Saviour.

The disciples, along with the first century believers, were five star Christians. The result was that they grew in the Lord Jesus, they had the favour of God on their lives, and the Lord added to the church daily.

In **Acts 2:41-47** we read that they continued steadfastly in the *"apostles' doctrine"*–that's **BIBLE**–*"and fellowship"*–that's **CHURCH**–*"and in prayers"*–that's **PRAYER**.

We also read that they *"sold their possessions and goods, and parted them to all men"*–that's **GIVING**. And last we read that they continued daily going *"from house to house"*–that's **WITNESSING**.

These five things–Bible, church, prayer, giving, and witnessing–are the five stars of the Christian life.

These five ingredients were found in the first generation of believers' lives, and these five stars are the same thing we must have for God's full blessing on our lives.

Becoming a five star Christian is a goal that all believers can achieve.

Someone has said, "It takes the same thing to *keep* something going that it took to *get* it going." One thing is true: if we want what they had, we must do what they did. Becoming a five star Christian is a goal that all believers can achieve.

Being a five star Christian means that we are doing these five things consistently. Remember, victory comes by doing these five things consistently. Failure and defeat can be traced to the neglect of one or more.

In the following pages, the five things are represented by five trees. Each tree has different fruit. As you will see in the drawings, the root of the tree produces certain fruit. If there is no root, there is no fruit.

Matthew 7:16 says, *"Ye shall know them by their fruits."* Those who are concerned about being their best, and helping *others* to be *their* best, should learn to identify the neglected root by the missing fruit.

"And they continued stedfastly
in the apostles' doctrine…"

Faithfulness in BIBLE READING

In *Acts 2:41-47* we read that the disciples and first century Christians continued steadfastly in the *"apostles' doctrine"*–that's **BIBLE**.

The first star in becoming a five star Christian is to read the Bible every day.

Acts 17:11 says, *"These were more noble than those in Thessalonica, in that they received the Word with all readiness of mind, and searched the scriptures daily, whether those things were so."*

Notice that they had *"readiness of mind"* and they *"searched the scriptures daily."* These are the key words in this verse.

Sometimes when I read my Bible, I have many things on my mind. That is why the psalmist said, *"O God, Thou art my God; **early** will I seek Thee"* (*Psalm 63:1*). Morning is a good time to read because we are just waking up, and our minds are clear.

We can be awake for only an hour, and already the busyness starts creeping in. We think about all that we need to do. We must have *"readiness of mind"* when we read our Bibles so that God can speak to us.

When I read for any length of time, my mind can start to wander. The Lord Jesus can help us to bring *"into captivity every thought to the obedience of Christ" (II Corinthians 10:5)*. We must guard our thoughts. The most brilliant people in the world can have only one thought at a time.

We need to have a readiness of mind and search the Scriptures daily. Spending time in God's Word daily will produce fruit in the believer's life. It will produce:

Faith in the Lord.

Spending time in God's Word will produce faith. *"Faith cometh by hearing, and hearing by the Word of God" (Romans 10:17)*.

It takes faith to claim God's promises. *"Faith is the substance of things hoped for" (Hebrews 11:1)*. Faith is believing God.

One of my granddaughters was riding in the car with us one very rainy day. The rain was coming down in sheets. To be honest, I was a little uneasy driving in the downpour.

My granddaughter was in the back seat coloring a page in her coloring book. I said to my wife, "Maybe we should build an ark." My granddaughter said, without lifting her head, "God promised He would never do that again." She had faith and knew that the rain would stop before the flood came. Where did that faith come from? It came from God's Word.

It takes faith to please God because *"without faith it is impossible to please Him"* **(Hebrews 11:6)**. The goal of the Christian life is to please God. The Lord Jesus said, *"I do always those things that please Him"* **(John 8:29)**.

The more time we spend in God's Word and meditating on it, the more our faith increases. We cannot grow in faith and ignore God's Word.

Direction for life.

Spending time in God's Word will give us direction for life. God will never lead us contrary to the teaching of His Word. If we are praying about a matter and seeking counsel to make a decision, the answer will be according to God's Word. God will never guide us opposite from His Word. That is a great truth we can trust.

Psalm 119:105 says, *"Thy Word is a lamp unto my feet, and a light unto my path."* God will show us the next step through His Word.

He is not going to reveal everything to us at once. We would like Him to give us a detailed map of our life, but that is not the way the Lord works. We have to take one step at a time. We take a step, and He shows us the next step. He will give us direction, but He will show us one step at a time.

One of my favorite verses for direction of life is *Psalm 143:8*. *"Cause me to hear Thy lovingkindness in the morning; for in Thee do I trust: cause me to know the way wherein I should walk; for I lift up my soul unto Thee."* God can cause us to know the way.

Life sometimes has detours. No one wants to take them, but they are on our journey. When on a detour, you always see things you would never see, and everyone is more alert for the next sign. When you get back on the main road, you have a grateful heart. God's Word will help you not to get lost on the detours of life.

Understanding in the working of the Lord.

Spending time in God's Word will produce understanding. The psalmist said, *"I understand more than the ancients, because I keep Thy precepts…Through Thy precepts I get understanding: therefore I hate every false way"* **(Psalm 119:100-104)**.

We can measure the maturity of people by how they understand. *I Corinthians 13:11* says, *"When I was a child, I spake as a child, I understood as a child, I thought as a child: but when I became a man, I put away childish things."* We cannot take people any further than they are willing to go. The more they understand about what God has done for them, the further they will go.

Understanding is like God turning on the light. The psalmist said, *"The entrance of Thy words giveth light; it giveth understanding unto the simple"* **(Psalm 119:130)**.

We can be reading our Bibles and all of a sudden one word or sentence comes alive. We can read the same Scripture several times and every time get something new out of it. That is the way the Lord works.

Deliverance from personal battles.

The Word of God has the power to deliver. ***Psalm 107:20*** says, *"He sent His Word, and healed them, and delivered them from their destructions."* Only the Lord knows what battles are ahead in life, and His Word can deliver from destruction.

Nowhere is this more clearly seen than in the life and ministry of our dear Saviour. In ***Luke 4:1-13***, He was *"forty days tempted of the devil."* The Lord Jesus defeated Satan by quoting Scripture. He simply said, *"It is written..."*

The secret to winning the victory in our personal battles is to know the Word of God. ***Hosea 4:6*** says, *"My people are destroyed for lack of knowledge."*

We can get deliverance if we will spend time in God's Word. *"Ye shall know the truth, and the truth shall make you free" (**John 8:32**).* *"Thy Word is truth" (**John 17:17**).*

God's Word has the power to renew our minds. It begins with our thought life, and then we are transformed according to ***Romans 12:2***.

"And be not conformed to this world: but be ye transformed by the renewing of your mind, that ye may prove what is that good, and acceptable, and perfect, will of God."

People need to have their thinking changed if they are going to act differently. ***Philippians 2:5*** says, *"Let this mind be in you, which was also in Christ Jesus."*

As God's Word changes our thinking, our actions follow suit, and we are delivered from destruction. ***Psalm 17:4*** says, *"By the Word of Thy lips I have kept me from the paths of the destroyer."*

Spiritual growth.

If we spend time every day in God's Word, we will grow spiritually. ***II Peter 3:18*** says, *"But* *grow in grace, and in the knowledge of our Lord and Saviour Jesus Christ."*

If we want to grow, we have to read our Bibles. *"As newborn babes, desire the sincere milk of the Word, that ye may grow thereby"* (**I Peter 2:2**).

A good test to see if we are growing spiritually is to gauge how we react to the pressures and difficulties of life. **II Peter 1:5-6** says, *"And beside this, giving all diligence, add to your faith...temperance."* Temperance is self-control. Being able to handle what the world throws at us is temperance.

Christians who spend time in God's Word will have all this fruit. Christians who neglect God's Word will experience lack of fruit.

The following tree illustrates what daily Bible reading produces in the believer's life. Spending time in God's Word will give us this fruit:

★ **Faith.** Do you have faith? Is your faith increasing?
★ **Direction.** Are you getting direction for your life?

★ **Understanding.** Is God giving you understanding?

★ **Deliverance.** Have you experienced deliverance from personal battles?

★ **Spiritual Growth.** Are you growing spiritually?

If any of these fruits are missing in your life, then you are neglecting the Bible. This tree helps us see, "No root, no fruit."

BIBLE READING

Romans 10:17 - *Faith in the Lord*

Psalm 119:105; Psalm 143:8 - *Direction for Life*

Psalm 119:100, 104 - *Understanding in the Working of the Lord*

Psalm 107:20 - *Deliverance from Personal Battles*

II Peter 3:8 - *Spiritual Growth*

Getting Started in BIBLE READING

★ Read God's Word daily.

I Timothy 4:13, *"Till I come, give attendance to reading, to exhortation, to doctrine."*

Revelation 1:3, *"Blessed is he that readeth, and they that hear the words of this prophecy, and keep those things which are written therein: for the time is at hand."*

✭ Read three chapters every day. This 30-day reading schedule will get you started. (Mark through the chapters as you read. Example: *John ~~1 2 3~~ 4 5...*)

John *1 2 3 4 5 6 7 8 9 10 11 12 13 14 15 16 17 18 19 20 21* *I Peter 1 2 3 4 5* *II Peter 1 2 3* *Philippians 1 2 3 4* *Psalm 1 27 119:1-56 119:57-112 119:113-176* *Romans 1 2 3 4 5 6 7 8 9 10 11 12 13 14 15 16* *I John 1 2 3 4 5* *II John 1* *III John 1* *Philemon 1* *Luke 1 2 3 4 5 6 7 8 9 10 11 12 13 14 15 16 17 18 19 20 21 22 23 24* *I Thessalonians 1 2 3 4*

★ Meditate on God's Word.

Joshua 1:8, *"This book of the law shall not depart out of thy mouth; but thou shalt meditate therein day and night, that thou mayest observe to do according to all that is written therein: for then thou shalt make thy way prosperous, and then thou shalt have good success."*

☆ The 19 references below have a total of 30 verses. Write out the verses on 3x5" cards to carry with you. Meditate on one verse each day. References with more than one verse cover two or three days depending on how many verses.

John *3:16* *8:29* *10:27-29* *11:25-26* *I Peter* *2:2* *5:7-8* *Philippians* *1:21* *4:13* *4:19* *Psalm* *1:1* *119:11* *119:105* *Romans* *8:28* *12:1-2* *I John* *1:9* *2:15-17* *3:1-3* *5:11-13* *Acts* *1:8*

★ Study God's Word.

II Timothy 2:15, *"Study to shew thyself approved unto God, a workman that needeth not to be ashamed, rightly dividing the word of truth."*

☆ Begin by faithfully attending Sunday School.

☆ As you grow, learn different methods of Bible study and read the great stories of the Bible.

☆ Make studying the Bible a lifetime habit.

These are the
five stars of the Christian life:

★   *Bible*

★   *Prayer*

★   *Church*

★   *Giving*

★   *Witnessing*

Victory comes by
doing these five things consistently.
Failure and defeat can be traced to
the neglect of one or more.

"And they continued stedfastly
...in prayers..."

$\mathcal{F}aithfulness$ in
PRAYER

The disciples, along with the first century believers, were five star Christians as they continued steadfastly *"in prayers."*

The second star in becoming a five star Christian is to develop a prayer life.

I love this verse. In ***Jeremiah 33:3*** God says, *"Call unto Me, and I will answer thee, and shew thee great and mighty things, which thou knowest not."* There is so much we do not know. God can show us great and mighty things if we will just pray and ask Him.

I have heard people say, "I don't have faith in my prayers anymore." I am reminded that it is not faith in my prayer, but it is *"the prayer of faith"* *(James 5:15-16)* that God answers. Our faith is not in our ability to pray, but in the One to whom we are praying.

We have a God who hears and answers prayer. **Matthew 7:7-8** says, *"Ask, and it shall be given you; seek, and ye shall find; knock, and it shall be opened unto you: For every one that asketh receiveth; and he that seeketh findeth; and to him that knocketh it shall be opened."*

Spending time daily in prayer will produce the following fruit:

Victory and spiritual growth in the lives of others.

Prayer produces victory. Our prayers are a vital part in winning the victory in the lives of others. If we pray for people, they will win personal victories. We have a responsibility as Christians to pray for one another.

Nothing encourages me more than to hear that others are praying for me. *"The effectual fervent prayer of a righteous man availeth much"* (**James 5:16**).

A lady asked me to pray for her and her children because she could not pray for them herself. She said she was not on praying ground. How sad. Her words stung me and surprised me. That is one thing I want in my life, to be able to pray for my family and for others.

We all need to be on praying ground by staying in fellowship with the Lord. Not only do *we* need the Lord's help, but *others* do also.

Colossians 1:9 says, *"For this cause we also, since the day we heard it, do not cease to pray for you, and to desire that ye might be filled with the knowledge of His will in all wisdom and spiritual understanding."* Whom have you prayed for that God has blessed?

I Timothy 2:1 says, *"I exhort therefore, that, first of all, supplications, prayers, intercessions, and giving of thanks, be made for all men."* The Bible commands us to pray for others.

We will never know the power of prayer if we do not have a personal prayer life.

In ***Acts 12:1-19*** we read that Peter was put in prison and was going to be killed. ***Acts 12:5*** tells us, *"Peter therefore was kept in prison: but prayer was made without ceasing of the church unto God for him."* Later in verse ***17*** Peter *"declared* *unto them how the Lord had brought him out of the prison."*

God's people prayed for Peter, and he was delivered. Victory came because God's people prayed. The angel brought Peter out of prison, but it was prayer that brought the angel.

Think of our missionaries who would be saddened to know that no one is praying for them. They have many difficulties on the mission field. They need our prayers. We have a responsibility to pray for them as they labor on foreign soil.

The blessing of God on our lives.

If we develop a personal prayer life, we will receive the blessing of God on our lives. ***James 4:2*** says, *"Ye lust, and have not: ye kill, and desire to have, and cannot obtain: ye fight and war, yet ye have not, because ye ask not."*

That is simple. The Lord does not mean that we will have everything we *want*, but rather everything we *need* for which we pray. We must learn to want our needs and not need our wants.

My brother and I were in a meeting together, and we met each other with our wives at the hotel. I had made my reservations at approximately the same time he had made his. Our rooms were on the same floor with the exact same amenities.

As we were all checking in at the same time, my sister-in-law noticed that my rate for the room was much less than my brother's. She is a wonderful Christian and was trying to figure out how to ask, "Why is his room less than ours?" (I jokingly thought, "They just like me more than my brother!")

When she asked, the lady said, "He *requested* a lower rate." Evelyn stood there processing all that was being said, and I could not help but laugh. Finally I said, "Will you give my brother the same rate as you gave me?" The lady answered, "Yes, if they want it."

She continued to check them in at the higher rate. My sister-in-law spoke up and said, "May I have the same rate as Tommy?"

The lady replied, "Yes, now that *you* have asked for it, I can give it to you." Apparently their policy was, "*You* don't get it until *you* ask."

I think we all agree with the Lord when He says, *"Ye have not, because ye ask not"* (**James 4:2**). If we ask the Lord for what we need, He will give it to us.

A closeness to the Lord.

A personal prayer life will bring a closeness to the Lord. *James 4:8* says, *"Draw nigh to God, and He will draw nigh to you."* This great verse teaches that if we take a step toward the Lord, He takes a step toward us. We must realize that if we desire to be closer to the Lord, it is our move first.

Tarry at a promise until God meets you there. It is true that if we are going to move God, we must be moved by God. We have to respond to the Word of God and the tug of the Holy Spirit in our lives.

> If we desire to be closer to the Lord, it is our move first.

We are close to the people we talk to. The more we talk, the closer we are. The same thing is true with the Lord. The more we talk to the Lord, the closer our relationship will become with Him. He is the *"Friend that sticketh closer than a brother"* (**Proverbs 18:24**).

Power in the preaching and teaching of God's Word.

If we develop a personal prayer life, we will have power in the preaching and teaching of God's Word. ***II Thessalonians 3:1*** says, *"Finally, brethren, pray for us, that the Word of the Lord may have free course, and be glorified, even as it is with you."*

I think often of Goldie Brown, one of our senior citizen ladies who went Home to be with the Lord. She prayed for me and for the preaching of God's Word, and it made a big difference.

We need to pray for power for those who preach and teach God's Word. Someone said, "Prayerless pews make powerless pulpits."

We need to pray for power as the Gospel is given. *"And when they had **prayed**, the place was shaken where they were assembled together; and they were all filled with the Holy Ghost, and they spake the Word of God with boldness…And with great **power** gave the apostles witness" **(Acts 4:31, 33)**.*

Prayer is powerful. ***James 5:16*** says, *"The effectual fervent prayer of a righteous man availeth much."* Prayer is the one weapon the devil cannot duplicate or counterfeit.

The Word of God would have more effect on the lives of people if we prayed for those who are teaching and preaching God's Word.

Defense against the devil.

If we develop a personal prayer life, we will have a defense against the devil. Part of the armor of God and weapon of our warfare is prayer.

Ephesians 6:11-18 begins with: *"Put on the whole armour of God, that ye may be able to stand against the wiles of the devil."* Then the Word of God lists the armor every believer should wear every day.

The last piece of armor on the list is: *"Praying always with all prayer and supplication in the Spirit, and watching thereunto with all perseverance and supplication for all saints."*

The Lord Jesus told Peter that Satan wanted to destroy him, but He also told Peter that He prayed for him. He said, *"Satan hath desired to have you, that he may sift you as wheat: But I have prayed for thee, that thy faith fail not: and when thou art converted, strengthen thy brethren"* (**Luke 22:31-32**). The Lord's prayer protected Peter.

How many people would be delivered if we would just pray for them? There are many people in our families and churches who need our prayers. They can be delivered if we will pray for them.

Romans 8:26 says, *"Likewise the Spirit also helpeth our infirmities: for we know not what we should pray for as we ought: but the Spirit itself maketh intercession for us with groanings which cannot be uttered."*

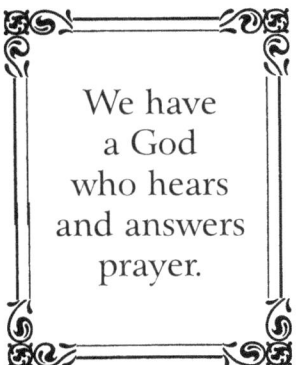

We have a God who hears and answers prayer.

We should ask the Holy Spirit to lead us in our requests to God. The Holy

Spirit will impress upon our minds and hearts what to say.

We need to have a daily prayer list and get serious about it. One day we will see how much we really prayed and cared for people.

Rewards in Heaven

Developing a personal prayer life gives us rewards in Heaven.

Our prayers are being kept in golden vials. **Revelation 5:8** says, *"And when He had taken the book, the four beasts and four and twenty elders fell down before the Lamb, having every one of them harps, and golden vials full of odours, which are the prayers of saints."*

Revelation 8:3-4 says, *"And another angel came and stood at the altar, having a golden censer; and there was given unto him much incense, that he should offer it with the prayers of all saints upon the golden altar which was before the throne.*

"And the smoke of the incense, which came with the prayers of the saints, ascended up before

These are the five stars of the Christian life:

* ✷ *Bible*
* ✷ *Prayer*
* ✷ *Church*
* ✷ *Giving*
* ✷ *Witnessing*

Victory comes by doing these five things consistently. Failure and defeat can be traced to the neglect of one or more.

God out of the angel's hand."

Our prayers will one day be offered to God as a testimony to how much we loved the Lord Jesus and how thankful we were that He blessed and cared for us. Will we rejoice when we see our prayers offered to the Lord?

Christians who spend time in prayer will have these fruits in their lives. Christians who do not will lack in these areas.

Following is the tree of prayer. The root is prayer. If we have a prayer life, it will produce:

★ **Victory and spiritual growth.**

★ **The blessing of God.**

★ **A closeness to the Lord.**

★ **Power in preaching and teaching God's Word.**

★ **Defense against the devil.**

★ **Rewards in Heaven.**

Do you have these fruits in your life? If you are missing any of these fruits, there is a problem with the root. The root is prayer. We must remember that to produce the fruit, we must have the root.

PRAYER

Victory

Closeness to the Lord

Blessings

Power

Defense Against
the Devil

Rewards
in Heaven

Prayer

I Timothy 2:1 - *Victory and Spiritual Growth in the Lives of Others*

Jeremiah 33:3 - *The Blessing of God on Our Lives*

James 4:8 - *A Closeness to the Lord*

II Thessalonians 3:1 - *Power in Preaching & Teaching God's Word*

Ephesians 6:11-18 - *Defense Against the Devil*

Revelation 5:8; 8:3,4 - *Rewards in Heaven*

Getting Started in PRAYER

★ Pray daily.

Psalm 55:17, *"Evening, and morning, and at noon, will I pray, and cry aloud: and He shall hear my voice."*

Psalm 86:3, *"Be merciful unto me, O Lord: for I cry unto Thee daily."*

★ Ask the Lord to help you live for Him.

Isaiah 41:10, *"Fear thou not; for I am with thee: be not dismayed; for I am thy God: I will strengthen thee; yea, I will help thee; yea, I will uphold thee with the right hand of My righteousness."*

★ Pray for the salvation of friends and loved ones.

Romans 9:2-3, *"That I have great heaviness and continual sorrow in my heart. For I could wish that myself were accursed from Christ for my brethren, my kinsmen according to the flesh."*

John 1:41-42, *"He first findeth his own brother…And he brought him to Jesus."*

★ Pray for those who preach and teach God's Word.

Ephesians 6:18-19, *"Praying always...for me, that utterance may be given unto me, that I may open my mouth boldly, to make known the mystery of the gospel."*

II Thessalonians 3:1, *"Finally, brethren, pray for us, that the word of the Lord may have free course, and be glorified, even as it is with you."*

★ Pray for your needs.

Philippians 4:19, *"But my God shall supply all your need according to His riches in glory by Christ Jesus."*

Date requested	Request	Date answered
_____	_____	_____
_____	_____	_____
_____	_____	_____
_____	_____	_____
_____	_____	_____
_____	_____	_____
_____	_____	_____
_____	_____	_____
_____	_____	_____
_____	_____	_____
_____	_____	_____
_____	_____	_____
_____	_____	_____

"And they continued stedfastly
in...fellowship..."

$\mathcal{F}aithfulness$ to
CHURCH

In *Acts 2:41-47* we read that the disciples continued steadfastly in *"fellowship"*–that's **CHURCH**.

The third star of becoming a five star Christian is being faithful to church.

Hebrews 10:24-25 says, *"And let us consider one another to provoke unto love and to good works: Not forsaking the assembling of ourselves together, as the manner of some is; but exhorting one another: and so much the more, as ye see the day approaching."*

Psalm 92:13 says, *"Those that be planted in the house of the LORD shall flourish in the courts of our God."*

These verses make it plain that God wants us in church.

*"Those that be **planted** in the house of the LORD shall flourish."* Faithfulness to church produces a *planted* Christian.

There is a difference between being a *planted* Christian and being a *potted* Christian. When a plant is in a pot, it can be taken out. There is no permanence. Neither is there room to grow. Pot-bound plants do not flourish; their roots are too crowded in the pot.

My wife, Nancy, always wanted to grow roses, so I bought her some rose bushes. She had several of them, all different colors, all so beautiful, all on our porch in pots. They were blooming at first, and she was babying them and having a great time.

Then they stopped producing roses, and the leaves began to wither and brown. I told her, "You are going to have to get them out of the pots, or they are going to die."

So she took them out of the pots and planted them in the yard. The only chance they had to live and grow was to be planted.

There are *planted* people, and there are *potted* people. Planted people are like the man in ***Psalm 1:3***.

*"And he shall be like a tree **planted** by the rivers of water, that bringeth forth his fruit in his season; his leaf also shall not wither; and whatsoever he doeth shall prosper."*

Potted people are carried away with every wind that blows. How sad that some Christians never get planted in a good church.

We must plant ourselves in the house of the Lord in order to flourish. Our roots will grow deeper and deeper, and we will become stronger and stronger. If we put our roots down in a good church, the Lord will bless our lives.

Encouragement in the believer's life.

Faithfulness to church produces encouragement in the life of the child of God. ***Hebrews 10:25*** says, *"Not forsaking the assembling of ourselves together, as the manner of some is; but exhorting one another: and so much the more, as ye see the day approaching."*

It is the will of God to encourage someone every day. ***Hebrews 3:13*** says, *"But exhort one another daily, while it is called To day; lest any of you be hardened through the deceitfulness of sin."*

What better place to encourage someone than in church. A pat on the back and a "That a boy!" go a long way in the work of the Lord.

The opposite of encouragement is discouragement. When people begin to miss church services, they become discouraged. Often they do not even realize what caused their discouragement. I have never met a Christian who was unfaithful to church who was not discouraged.

Fellowship with God's people.

Faithfulness to church provides fellowship with God's people. Church is a fellowship of believers who have joined together to accomplish God's plan and purpose. Fellowship is one of the glues that holds a church together. It is a spirit of one accord.

We cannot have fellowship with people if we are not in one accord with them. *I John 1:7* says, *"But if we walk in the light, as He is in the light, we have fellowship one with another, and the blood of Jesus Christ His Son cleanseth us from all sin."* How can we have fellowship with one another if we are not walking in the same light?

Christians whose spouses are not saved have such difficulty because they are not walking in the same light, and it is hard for them to have fellowship. They cannot have the kind of fellowship the Lord wants them to have. It is the same with all Christians who have unsaved family members or friends.

Acts 2:42 says, *"And they continued stedfastly in the apostles' doctrine and **fellowship**, and in breaking of bread, and in prayers."* We need fellowship with other Christians, and that need is met in the church.

Dr. Lee Roberson says, "It takes three to thrive: Sunday morning, Sunday night, and Wednesday night."

Protection from the world, the flesh, and the devil.

The devil recognized that God put a hedge around Job and his family. In **Job 1:10** Satan said to God, *"Hast not Thou made an hedge about him, and about his house, and about all that he hath on every side?"*

The church has a hedge of protection. The Lord Jesus promised, *"I will build My church; and the gates of hell shall not prevail against it"* **(Matthew 16:18)**.

In *Luke 22:32*, the Lord Jesus told Simon Peter that Satan had desired to have him and destroy him, but He said, *"I have prayed for thee."* There is protection in God's family.

The safest place for us and for our families is in a strong church. Many Christians have been devoured because they left a good church. A strong church is the safest place we can be.

Asaph said that he did not fully understand the destruction and power of the world, the flesh, and the devil until he went to the house of God. *"Until I went into the sanctuary of God; then understood I their end" (Psalm 73:17).*

Opportunity to have a part in the Lord's work.

Faithfulness to the local church provides opportunity for us to have a part in the Lord's work. The Bible says to *"commit"* the work of the Lord *"to faithful men" (II Timothy 2:2).*

There is a job for everyone in the local church. One day *"every man's work shall be made manifest: ...and the fire shall try every man's work of what sort it is" (I Corinthians 3:13).* Since *"every man's work"* will be judged, we know there is a work for every man.

We must be faithful in order to have a part in the Lord's work. God is not going to use people unless they are faithful. We may not be able to do many things, but one thing we all can do is to be faithful.

Revelation 2:10 says, *"Be thou faithful unto death, and I will give thee a crown of life."* God wants us to be faithful.

The joy of the Lord.

Church has a rejoicing spirit. Have you ever been really "down," but coming to church picked you up? That is the Lord giving you joy. God promises in **Isaiah 56:7** that He will *"make them joyful in My house of prayer."*

In **Psalm 42:4** the psalmist testifies, *"I had gone with the multitude, I went with them to the house of God, with the voice of joy and praise."*

The first century Christians continued *"daily with one accord in the temple, and...from house to house, ...with **gladness** and singleness of heart"* (**Acts 2:46**). They were happy people.

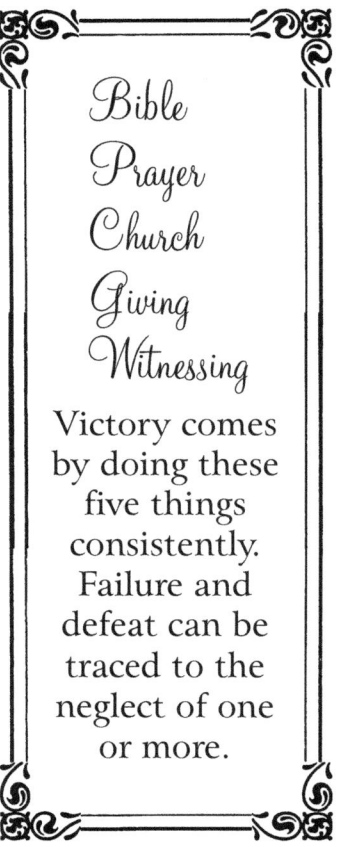

Bible

Prayer

Church

Giving

Witnessing

Victory comes by doing these five things consistently. Failure and defeat can be traced to the neglect of one or more.

The happiest people in the world are God's people. ***Nehemiah 8:10*** tells us *"the joy of the LORD is your strength."*

No wonder David said, *"I was glad when they said unto me, Let us go into the house of the LORD"* ***(Psalm 122:1)***.

Look at the fruit on the next tree. Christians who are faithful to church will have this fruit. Christians who neglect being faithful to church will experience lack in these areas.

Faithfulness to church produces:

★ **Encouragement for the Christian life.**

★ **Fellowship with God's people.**

- ★ **Protection from the world, the flesh, and the devil.**
- ★ **Opportunity for Christian service.**
- ★ **Joy in the believer's life.**

If any of this fruit is missing in your life, check the root of it, which is faithfulness to church. If you want the fruit, you have to have the root.

CHURCH

Fellowship
Protection
Joy
Encouragement
Opportunity
Church

Hebrews 10:25 - *Encouragement in the Believer's Life*

I John 1:7; Acts 2:42 - *Fellowship with God's People*

Psalm 42:4 - *The Joy of the Lord*

Job 1:10; Luke 22:32 - *Protection from the World, the Flesh, and the Devil*

II Timothy 2:2 - *Opportunity to Have a Part in the Lord's Work*

Getting Started in CHURCH

Put your life and family in a good church and determine to be faithful. ***Acts 2:47***, *"The Lord added to the church daily."*

★ **Attend every service of your church.**

Hebrews 10:25, *"Not forsaking the assembling of ourselves together, ...but exhorting one another: and so much the more, as ye see the day approaching."*

Psalm 111:1, *"Praise ye the* LORD. *I will praise the* LORD *with my whole heart, in the assembly of the upright, and in the congregation."*

★ **Be a part of Sunday School where the Word of God is taught.**

I Timothy 3:15, *"That thou mayest know how thou oughtest to behave thyself in the house of God, which is the church of the living God, the pillar and ground of the truth."*

★ **Faithfully attend special meetings.**

Psalm 122:1, *"I was glad when they said unto me, Let us go into the house of the* LORD."*

"And sold their possessions and goods,
and parted them to all men..."

Faithfulness in GIVING

We read in *Acts 2:41-47* that the disciples and first century Christians *"sold their possessions and goods, and parted them to all men"*–that's **GIVING**.

The fourth star in the five star Christian life is giving. The disciples along with the first generation Christians were faithful in giving and even sold their possessions in order to give to the cause of Christ.

There are three levels of giving:

FIRST, there is the tithe. The tithe belongs to the Lord. It is His, not ours. That is why the Bible says we are to *"bring ye all the tithes into the storehouse" (Malachi 3:10)*. The tithe is 10% of our income, and it belongs to the Lord, so we are to *"bring"* it to Him. When we bring the tithe, God does some wonderful things for us as we shall see in this chapter.

SECOND, there is giving above the tithe. This giving is called *"offerings"* and comes out of the 90% we have left after the tithe. We will also see that God blesses those who give above the tithe.

So we are to *"bring"* our *"tithes"* and give our *"offerings."* Tithing is not giving, and giving is not tithing.

A dear friend of mine was telling me about his first job. He was a teenager and had made twenty dollars. His Christian mother sat down with him and asked, "What belongs to God?" My friend said he took two dollars and set them aside.

Then she asked, "What are you going to give the Lord?" He said, "Here is my offering, these two dollars." She said, "That is not yours, that is the Lord's. Your offering comes out of the eighteen dollars you have left after the tithe." My friend told me that was one of the greatest lessons he has ever learned about giving.

THIRD, there is faith giving. This is God giving through us. All who understand the great need in the Lord's work have a desire to do more but find it humanly impossible. God honors our faith and desire, and He brings unexpected blessings into our lives. The Lord is always looking for someone whom He can bless and give through, someone whom He can make a channel of blessing.

God knows how to provide *for* His children, and He knows how to give *through* His children. We need to trust Him. God says, *"Bring ye all the tithes into the storehouse...and prove Me...if I will not open you the windows of heaven, and pour you out a blessing" (**Malachi 3:10**)*. We must take that step of faith in our giving.

Too many people hit and miss when it comes to giving. They start, and they stop. It is like taking medicine. The doctor says, "Take the whole bottle." Sometimes we decide, "Well, I don't need this anymore," so we quit taking it, and then we have a relapse. We should know better. Neither can we hit and miss at giving.

We have to be faithful in giving long enough for it to take root. People do not get in the condition they are in overnight, and they do not get out overnight, but they must begin somewhere.

We must be faithful to God. *I Corinthians 4:2* says, *"Moreover it is required in stewards, that a man be found faithful."*

Faithfulness in giving produces fruit in our lives. It produces:

Open windows of Heaven in our lives.

If we are faithful in bringing the tithe, God opens the windows of Heaven in our lives. *Malachi 3:10* says, *"Bring ye all the tithes into the storehouse, that there may be meat in Mine house, and prove Me now herewith, saith the* LORD *of hosts, if I will not open you the windows of heaven, and pour you out a blessing, that there shall not be room enough to receive it."* The Lord is asking us to give Him an opportunity to do something wonderful in our lives.

Do *you* have the windows of Heaven open in *your* life? God sends blessings through those windows. If you have the windows open a tiny crack, that is how little the Lord can bless you. If you have the windows open wide, the Lord can bless you so much more.

I heard an old preacher say, "I have learned that the hole I give through is the same hole God gives through to me. I want to make it big."

Defense against the devil.

Faithfulness in tithing produces a defense against the devil. In **Malachi 3:11**, the Lord says, *"And I will rebuke the devourer for your sakes, and he shall not destroy the fruits of your ground."* When we tithe, the Lord rebukes the devourer.

The devil is the devourer. **I Peter 5:8** says, *"Be sober, be vigilant; because your adversary the devil, as a roaring lion, walketh about, seeking whom he may devour."*

To *"devour"* means to make disappear. The devil is real, and he wants to devour us and our families. I want the Lord to rebuke him, don't you?

Do we believe the devil is real? We say we do, but do we really act like it? Tithing provides defense against the devil, and we need it.

Protection of our fruit.

Faithfulness in tithing will produce the protection of our fruit. ***Malachi 3:11*** continues, *"Neither shall your vine cast her fruit before the time in the field, saith the* LORD *of hosts."*

What is the fruit of our lives? It is what we have accomplished in our lives, our families, our work, our ministry, our testimonies. All these are the fruits of our lives. If we faithfully tithe, the Lord says He will protect our fruit. It would be a very unwise farmer who did not protect his fruit.

The blessings from others on our lives.

Faithfulness in giving produces the blessings from others on our lives. When we give, the Lord causes others to be a blessing to us.

He says in ***Luke 6:38***, *"Give, and it shall be given unto you; good measure, pressed down, and shaken together, and running over, shall men give into your bosom. For with the same measure that ye mete withal it shall be measured to you again."*

God speaks to the hearts of people about being a blessing to us. When we review our lives, we will see how the Lord allowed our paths to cross the paths of others who blessed us.

Treasures in Heaven.

When we are faithful in giving, it produces treasures in Heaven. ***Matthew 6:20-21*** says, *"But lay up for yourselves treasures in heaven, where neither moth nor rust doth corrupt, and where thieves do not break through nor steal. For where your treasure is, there will your heart be also."* The Lord says that where our treasure is, there our heart is also.

God will bless us for giving even a cup of water to a little one. ***Matthew 10:42*** says, *"And whosoever shall give to drink unto one of these little ones a cup of cold water only in the name of a disciple, verily I say unto you, he shall in no wise lose his reward."* Our reward is *"reserved in heaven"* (***I Peter 1:4***).

What we give can be used to reach others with the Gospel and provide an opportunity for the Lord to work. I like the expression that I heard years ago that says, "I'm giving while I'm living so I'm knowing where it's going."

Next we see the tree of giving. Christians who are faithful in giving will have this fruit. Christians who are not faithful will experience lack in these areas. Remember, when there is no root, there is no fruit.

Look at the tree of giving. This is what faithfulness in giving produces.

> ★ **Windows of Heaven opened.**
> ★ **Defense against the devil.**
> ★ **Protection of our fruit.**
> ★ **Blessings from others.**
> ★ **Treasures in Heaven.**

Look at all the fruit produced if we are just faithful in giving to the Lord.

GIVING

Malachi 3:10 - *The Windows of Heaven Opened in Our Lives*

Luke 6:38 - *The Blessing from Others on Our Lives*

Malachi 3:11; I Peter 5:8 - *Defense Against the Devil*

Matthew 6:20; 10:42; I Peter 1:4 - *Treasures in Heaven*

Malachi 3:11 - *Protection of Our Fruit*

Getting Started in GIVING

Determine to be a faithful steward.

I Corinthians 4:2, *"Moreover it is required in stewards, that a man be found faithful."*

★ Be a tither.

Malachi 3:10, *"Bring ye all the tithes into the storehouse, that there may be meat in Mine house, and prove Me now herewith, saith the LORD of hosts, if I will not open you the windows of heaven, and pour you out a blessing, that there shall not be room enough to receive it."*

★ Give above the tithe.

Luke 6:38, *"Give, and it shall be given unto you; good measure, pressed down, and shaken together, and running over, shall men give into your bosom. For with the same measure that ye mete withal it shall be measured to you again."*

★ Ask God to increase your faith in the area of giving.

II Corinthians 8:3-5, *"...Beyond their power they were willing of themselves; ...but first gave their own selves to the Lord, and unto us by the will of God."*

☆ ☆ ☆ ☆ ☆ ☆ ☆ ☆ ☆ ☆ ☆ ☆ ☆ ☆

These are the
five stars of the Christian life:

★   *Bible*

★   *Prayer*

★   *Church*

★   *Giving*

★   *Witnessing*

Victory comes by
doing these five things consistently.
Failure and defeat can be traced to
the neglect of one or more.

"And they continued stedfastly
...from house to house..."

Faithfulness in WITNESSING

The fifth and final star in the five star Christian life is witnessing.

The disciples, along with the first century believers, were five star Christians. ***Acts 2:41-47*** says that they continued daily going *"from house to house"*–that's **WITNESSING**.

In ***Acts 1:8***, the Lord Jesus said, *"But ye shall receive power, after that the Holy Ghost is come upon you: and **ye shall be witnesses unto Me** both in Jerusalem, and in all Judaea, and in Samaria, and unto the uttermost part of the earth."*

Every generation of believers is responsible to reach their generation with the Gospel. Everyone who gets saved is a result of someone's witness.

In ***Ezekiel 3:17-18****,* God says, *"I have made thee a watchman...to warn the wicked from his wicked way, to save his life."*

One day we will see the sad ending of those who die without Christ (***Revelation 20:15***). The most heart-breaking day in all human history will be the day of the Great White Throne Judgment. Imagine people being separated from God for ever.

We have a great responsibility. We need to be faithful to the Lord in witnessing.

Witnessing produces fruit in a believer's life.

Joy in Heaven.

Witnessing produces joy in Heaven. ***Luke 15:10*** says, *"Likewise, I say unto you, there is joy in the presence of the angels of God over one sinner that repenteth."* When one person gets saved, there is rejoicing in Heaven.

It is important for us to be happy too when someone gets saved. We should rejoice. God is so good to allow us to have a part in someone's salvation! Seeing someone saved as a result of our witness brings great joy.

I remember the first person that came to Christ as a result of my witness. My pastor, Dick Riley, helped me find a place of service in our church and gave me an opportunity to serve the Lord Jesus in the bus ministry.

One Saturday evening, I was visiting a man and his children who had just started riding our Sunday School bus. He lived in a mobile home park full of boys and girls.

As I left his home, I noticed a young girl and her mother sitting on their front patio. (I later learned that this young mother had recently lost her husband in a terrible accident.)

I walked over to her patio and invited her and her little girl to ride our bus to Sunday School. She took the Gospel tract I offered and asked me a very interesting question. She said, "What does your church believe?"

Now, I was a babe in Christ and did not know much about the Bible and church, but I knew what had happened in my life, so I said, "Our church believes in getting people saved."

Then she asked me a question that scared me to death. She said, "How do people get saved?"

I had just recently come to Christ myself and had never told someone else how to be saved, but I had a little booklet given to me by my pastor titled, "New Steps in the Right Direction." It had a chapter on how to know Christ as your personal Saviour.

When I went to my car to get the little booklet that I had been reading, I asked the Lord to help me.

I took that booklet and read word for word the chapter on knowing Christ. When I got to the prayer, I told her that it was like the prayer I had prayed, and invited her to pray.

It stirs my heart as I recall how sweetly those two prayed that night on their patio. The Lord's presence was so real that we were all weeping.

She promised she would come to Sunday School the next morning.

When I got in my car to go home, I could not hold back the tears of joy. God did something in my heart that night that I never want to lose.

When our bus arrived at her home the next morning, she was standing on the front patio with her little girl and four other children that she had rounded up.

The Lord did a wonderful work in that mobile home park through that family.

I have since learned much more about witnessing, but the one thing that we must do to have joy is to tell what the Lord Jesus has done for us.

Rewards at the Judgment Seat of Christ.

Witnessing produces rewards at the Judgment Seat of Christ. The Apostle Paul said to those he had won to Christ, *"For what is our hope, or joy, or crown of rejoicing? Are not even ye in the presence of our Lord Jesus Christ at His coming? For ye are our glory and joy"* **(I Thessalonians 2:19-20)**.

The crown of rejoicing is given to those who are faithful witnesses. Every Christian can receive the soul winner's crown.

Proverbs 11:30 tells us, *"He that winneth souls is wise."* *"And they that be wise shall shine as the brightness of the firmament; and they that turn many to righteousness as the stars for ever and ever"* **(Daniel 12:3)**.

Imagine what happens when a faithful witness arrives in Heaven. People rejoice to see the one who led them to the Lord. There will be rewards at the Judgment Seat of Christ.

Compassion in a believer's life.

In **Matthew 9:35-36**, the Bible says, *"And Jesus went about all the cities and villages, teaching in their synagogues, and preaching the gospel of the kingdom, and healing every sickness and every disease among the people. But when He saw the multitudes, He was moved with compassion on them, because they fainted, and were scattered abroad, as sheep having no shepherd."*

Seeing the multitudes of people moved the Lord; He had compassion on them. Seeing people where they are changes our lives.

We do not get compassion by thinking about it or praying about it. Compassion comes when we go and see. *"Jesus went...He saw the multitudes,"* and *"He was moved with compassion on them."*

Compassion is having people in our hearts.

Some of the greatest truths I ever learned were when I was a Sunday School bus captain and saw the condition of people without the Lord.

We all have problems, things that we deal with every day, heartaches and burdens we are bearing. But witnessing, visiting, and seeing people puts it all in perspective.

Compassion is not just having people's problems in our hearts; it is having people in our hearts. We get compassion by getting out there and being among people. This is the only way to get compassion. Compassion changes people's lives.

Vision for the work of the Lord.

Faithfulness in witnessing produces vision for the work of the Lord. ***Matthew 9:37-38*** says, *"Then saith He unto His disciples, The harvest truly is plenteous, but the labourers are few; Pray ye therefore the Lord of the harvest, that He will send forth labourers into His harvest."*

Vision is seeing people the way the Lord sees them.

Proverbs 29:18 tells us, *"Where there is no vision, the people perish."* But the Lord is *"not willing that any should perish"* (***II Peter 3:9***), so He gives us a vision for the lost.

Vision is seeing people the way the Lord sees them. We must first see people in their lost condition before the Lord will show us how to reach them. Then as we go, God shows us how to make a difference in people's lives. *"Some have compassion, making a difference"* (***Jude 1:22***).

Remember that the Lord Jesus promised, *"Lo, I am with you alway."* His presence with us as we witness helps us see the great need.

May the Lord help all who read this book to *"lift up your eyes, and look on the fields; for they are white already to harvest" (**John 4:35**)*. Ask God to help you make a difference in people's lives.

Victory in the believer's life.

Another fruit that is produced by faithfulness in witnessing is victory in the believer's life. We sing a song that I love which says, "I'm on the winning side." We can be on the winning side. We can have victory in the Lord.

The Christian life is a life of victory. *"Thanks be to God, which giveth us the victory through our Lord Jesus Christ" (**I Corinthians 15:57**)*.

One of my favorite verses is **Matthew 1:21.** *"And she shall bring forth a Son, and thou shalt call His name JESUS* (that means Saviour)*: for He shall save His people* (that means Christians) *from their sins."*

The Lord Jesus saves us, and then He delivers us. One of the ways He delivers us from the practice of sin is by His presence.

He tells us to *"go"* to where people are and tell them how to know Him. And He says *"Lo, I am with you" (Matthew 28:19-20).*

As we go and tell others what the Lord has done in our lives, He goes with us. It is in His presence that we win the victory.

I remember as a new Christian (I was saved when I was twenty-six), how the Lord Jesus delivered me from smoking. As a new Christian I struggled with many things, but smoking was the biggest battle I was fighting. I knew that it was not healthy and that Christians should not smoke, but it had a grip on me.

I even had a man I worked with tell me not to talk to him about being a Christian "with those things in your shirt pocket." I learned that cigarettes and Gospel tracts cannot go in the same pocket. I was stung by his rebuke, but I did not quit.

I was becoming a closet smoker. By that I mean that I would not smoke around church members or other Christians I knew. But when church was over, I would run out, get in my car, and head home so that I could have a cigarette. By the time church was over, I was having a nicotine fit. I used breath mints and sprays to hide the smell, but I am sure no one was fooled.

The Christian life is a life of victory.

My wife and I dedicated our home to the Lord, and we were reading the Bible and praying daily in our home. She told me that because we had given our home to the Lord, I had to smoke outside. She had me convinced that God would either kill me or do something terrible to me if I smoked in our house. So I smoked outside in front of our house.

Here I was. I could not smoke in my house, on the job, or at church. God was putting me in a corner, but I still did not have the victory.

My pastor encouraged me to memorize the Scriptures and to witness to others. I knew not to take my cigarettes on visitation because it was not becoming as a Christian, and I was convicted about it. But one day something happened that changed my life and delivered me from that bad habit.

I was memorizing the Great Commission as found in *Matthew 28:19-20*. I will never forget when God opened my eyes to the truth in the last part of that verse: *"Lo, I am with you."* I realized that the Lord Jesus was with me.

I had been hiding my smoking from my pastor and my Christian friends. I was even hiding my smoking from the unsaved people that I worked with. But I could not hide from the Lord. He was with me.

He manifests His presence when we witness. It is *"for this purpose the Son of God was manifested, that He might destroy the works of the devil" (I John 3:8)*.

It is in His presence that we win the victory. He promises to go with us as we witness to others.

Look at the tree of witnessing. Faithfulness in witnessing produces:

> ★ **Joy in Heaven.**
> ★ **Rewards at the Judgment Seat of Christ.**
> ★ **Compassion for others.**

★ **Vision for the Lord's work.**

★ **Victory in the Christian life.**

If you want the fruit, you have to have the root. No witnessing causes lack of this fruit.

WITNESSING

Rewards

Compassion

Vision

Joy

Victory

Witnessing

Luke 15:10 - *Joy in Heaven*

I Thessalonians 2:19-20; Daniel 12:3; Proverbs 11:30 - *Rewards at the Judgment Seat of Christ*

Matthew 9:35-36 - *Compassion in a Believer's Life*

Matthew 9:37-38; John 4:35 - *Vision for the Work of the Lord*

Matthew 28:19-20; I John 3:8 - *Victory in the Believer's Life*

Getting Started in
WITNESSING

★ **Carry Gospel tracts.**

Matthew 5:16, *"Let your light so shine before men, that they may see your good works, and glorify your Father which is in heaven."*

★ **Share your testimony.**

Psalm 107:2, *"Let the redeemed of the LORD say so."*

★ **Invite friends, loved ones, and those you meet to church.**

Luke 14:23, *"And the Lord said unto the servant, Go out into the highways and hedges, and compel them to come in, that My house may be filled."*

★ **Learn how to win souls.**

Proverbs 11:30, *"He that winneth souls is wise."*

Acts 26:22, *"Having therefore obtained help of God, I continue unto this day, witnessing both to small and great."*

★ Be active in church outreach.

Matthew 28:18-20, *"And Jesus came and spake unto them, saying, All power is given unto Me in heaven and in earth. Go ye therefore, and teach all nations, baptizing them in the name of the Father, and of the Son, and of the Holy Ghost: Teaching them to observe all things whatsoever I have commanded you: and, lo, I am with you alway, even unto the end of the world. Amen."*

These are the
five stars of the Christian life:

★   *Bible*

★   *Prayer*

★   *Church*

★   *Giving*

★   *Witnessing*

Victory comes by
doing these five things consistently.
Failure and defeat can be traced to
the neglect of one or more.

The disciples, along with the first century believers,
were five star Christians.
The result was that they grew in the Lord Jesus,
they had the favour of God on their lives,
and the Lord added to the church daily.

Being a
FIVE STAR CHRISTIAN

As we have read in *Acts 2:41-47*, the disciples and first century believers were five star Christians. They continued steadfastly in:

- ★ **Daily Bible reading.**
- ★ **Prayer.**
- ★ **Faithfulness to church.**
- ★ **Giving.**
- ★ **Witnessing.**

Christians are made strong as a result of doing these five things consistently, but they will have weakness and a lack of fruit in their lives as a result of neglecting any of these five things.

As we look at the last tree, look at all the fruit! If we want all the fruit, we must have all the roots. Determine to become a five star Christian.

These are the
five stars of the Christian life:

★   *Bible*

★   *Prayer*

★   *Church*

★   *Giving*

★   *Witnessing*

Victory comes by
doing these five things consistently.
Failure and defeat can be traced to
the neglect of one or more.

BEING A FIVE STAR CHRISTIAN

Understanding

Protection

Encouragement

Compassion

Closeness

Defense

Opportunity

Direction

Power

Victory

Fellowship

Rewards

Blessings

Windows of

Spiritual

Deliverance

Joy

Heaven Opened

Growth

Treasures

Faith

Vision

Daily Bible Reading

Prayer

Church

Giving

Witnessing

My Commitment to Become a
FIVE STAR CHRISTIAN

With God as my helper, I commit my life to do these five things and become a five star Christian.

★ DAILY BIBLE READING

II Timothy 2:15, *"Study to shew thyself approved unto God, a workman that needeth not to be ashamed, rightly dividing the word of truth."*

Psalm 119:11, *"Thy Word have I hid in mine heart, that I might not sin against Thee."*

★ PRAYER

I Thessalonians 5:17, *"Pray without ceasing."*

Philippians 4:6, *"In every thing by prayer and supplication with thanksgiving let your requests be made known unto God."*

★ FAITHFULNESS TO CHURCH

Hebrews 10:25, *"Not forsaking the assembling of ourselves together."*

Acts 2:42, *"And they continued stedfastly in... fellowship."*

★ GIVING

Malachi 3:10, *"Bring ye all the tithes into the storehouse."*

Luke 6:38, *"Give, and it shall be given unto you."*

II Corinthians 8:3, *"Beyond their power they were willing of themselves."*

★ WITNESSING

Romans 1:16, *"For I am not ashamed of the gospel of Christ: for it is the power of God unto salvation to every one that believeth."*

Signed: _____

Dated: _____

"For God so loved the world, that He gave His only begotten Son, that whosoever believeth in Him should not perish, but have everlasting life."

John 3:16

Everlasting Life Can Be Yours

"For God so loved the world, that He gave His only begotten Son, that whosoever believeth in Him should not perish, but have everlasting life."
John 3:16

This great verse reveals four precious truths from the heart of God.

You are loved.

God wants you to know that **you are loved**. The Lord Jesus said, *"For God so loved the world."* You are a part of this world, and God loves you.

You are of worth.

The Lord also wants you to know that **you are of worth**. You are so dear to God that *"He gave His only begotten Son."* He gave His Son, Jesus Christ, to pay your sin debt.

The Bible teaches us that we are all sinners. *"For all have sinned, and come short of the glory of God" (**Romans 3:23**).* And sin must be paid for. *"For the wages of sin is death" (**Romans 6:23**).*

The good news is that the Lord Jesus paid our sin debt in full when He died on the cross. *"For He hath made Him to be sin for us" (**II Corinthians 5:21**).*

Christ's payment for our sin was accepted by God. It satisfied God's requirement for forgiveness.

You may ask, "How can God forgive sin?" He can because of what Jesus did for us. *"While we were yet sinners, Christ died for us" (**Romans 5:8**).*

You can have hope.

God wants you to know that **you can have hope**. He said *"that whosoever believeth in Him should not perish."*

The Lord does not want anyone to be separated from God. We were created to spend eternity with Him.

You can have purpose.

God wants you to know that **you can have purpose** in life. He desires that you *"should not perish but have everlasting life."*

Everlasting life is ours when we turn to God in repentance and faith and receive the Lord Jesus Christ as our personal Saviour.

You may ask, "How do I do this?" The answer is as simple as ABC.

Acknowledge that you are a sinner, *"for all have sinned, and come short of the glory of God." - **Romans 3:23**.*

Believe that the Lord Jesus died for you, for *"Christ died for our sins according to the scriptures." - **I Corinthians 15:3**.*

Call upon the Lord to save you, *"for whosoever shall call upon the name of the Lord shall be saved." - **Romans 10:13**.*

If you would like to call on the Lord to save you, and have the promise of everlasting life, pray this prayer and receive Christ today.

*L*ORD, I know that I am a sinner, and I believe You died and rose again for me. I am trusting You to forgive me. Come into my heart and save me, and help me to live for You. In Jesus' name, Amen.

Everlasting life begins when we receive Christ as our personal Saviour.

The Lord Jesus said, *"And I give unto them eternal life; and they shall never perish"* (**John 10:28**).

Now that you have received the Lord Jesus as your personal Saviour, please contact us or the person who gave you this book. We would like to rejoice with you in your new-found faith.

WordToTheWorld@aol.com

www.FiveStarChristianMinistries.com